EVERYTHING THERE IS TO KNOW ABOUT THE VIETNAM WAR

History Facts Books

Children's War & Military Books

BABY PROFESSOR
EDUCATION KIDS

Speedy Publishing LLC
40 E. Main St. #1156
Newark, DE 19711
www.speedypublishing.com
Copyright 2017

The Vietnam War took place from November 1, 1955 through April 30, 1975 and was fought between the government of Southern Vietnam and communist North Vietnam. North Vietnam had the support of communist countries, including the Soviet Union and the People's Republic of China. South Vietnam had the support of anti-communist countries, consisting primarily of the United States. In this book, we will be learning about the war and how it affected the entire world.

PRIOR TO THE WAR

Before World War II, Vietnam had been a French colony and it was during WWII that the Japanese took over control of this area. Once the war ended, it had created a power vacuum. Communist and Vietnamese revolutionary Ho Chi Minh wanted the country to be free. The Allies all agreed, however, that Vietnam still belonged to France.

HO CHI MINH STATUE

HO CHI MINH IN DONG KHE

CONTAINMENT

Ho Chi Minh, along with his rebels, eventually starting fighting with the French. His soldiers in the north were named the Viet Minh. He attempted to get assistance from the United States, but they did not want him to be successful because they were concerned about spreading communism throughout Southeast Asia. Once Ho started having success against the French, the United States became even more concerned and they started sending aid to the French in 1950.

THE US ENTERS WAR

The French would lose a key battle to the Vietnamese in 1954 and decided it was time to pull out. The country was now divided into a Southern Vietnam and a communist Northern Vietnam and was supposed to reunite in 1956 under a single election. The US, however, did not want it to become a communist country and assisted in getting Ngo Dinh Diem elected in the South.

NGO DINH DIEM

VIETNAM WAR PROTESTERS

MAJOR EVENTS DURING THE WAR

- March 1959 - Ho Chi Minh declared all-out war in order to unite Vietnam under one rule.

- December 1961 - US military advisors begin to take a direct role in the war.

- August 1964 - The Gulf of Tonkin Resolution is passed by the US Congress after two US Destroyers were attacked by the North Vietnamese. This allowed US troops to use armed force in the area.

• March 8, 1965 - The first official US combat troops arrive in Vietnam. The US begins a bombing campaign of Northern Vietnam called Operation Rolling Thunder.

THE B-52 BOMBER WAS FIRST USED
IN VIETNAM IN JUNE 1965

January 30, 1968 - North Vietnam launches the
Tet Offensive attacking around 100 cities in
Southern Vietnam.

RICHARD NIXON

- July 1969 - President Nixon begins the withdrawal of US troops.

- March 1972 - The North Vietnamese attack across the border in the Easter Offensive.

PRESIDENT LYNDON JOHNSON'S PLAN

President Johnson had developed a plan to help strengthen the Southern Vietnamese so they could fight the North other than having the United States win the war for them. In placing limits on their troops and not permitting them to attack North Vietnam from 1965 to 1969, there was no chance for the United States to win.

LYNDON JOHNSON

U.S. MARINES IN OPERATION ALLEN BROOK

THE VIETNAM WAR WAS A DIFFICULT WAR

Not only were the Vietnam jungles a difficult place to fight a war, President Johnson had placed strategic limits on the US troops. It was quite difficult in the jungles to find the enemy as well as determining who was the enemy. They had to deal with constant ambushes and booby traps from the same people they were fighting for.

THE UNITED STATES EXITS THE WAR

Once Richard Nixon became president, he made the decision to end the involvement of the US in this war. In July of 1969, he started to remove troops from Vietnam and a cease fire was negotiated on January 27, 1973. In March of 1973, only a few months later, the final US troops left Vietnam.

AN AMERICAN SOLDIER DURING VIETNAM WAR

THE FLAG OF THE VIET CONG, ADOPTED IN 1960, IS A VARIATION ON THE FLAG OF NORTH VIETNAM

S outh Vietnam then surrendered to North Vietnam in April of 1975. The country soon officially became unified as the Socialist Republic of Vietnam and now was a communist country.

UH-1D_HELICOPTERS_IN_VIETNAM_1966

T he United States had now lost the Vietnam War as well as taken a major blow in the Cold War.

AN AMERICAN SOLDIER DURING VIETNAM WAR

WHO WON THE VIETNAM WAR?

After American troops withdrew in 1973, South Vietnam was taken over completely by communist forces in 1975, which meant the end of the war and victory for the Communists. Therefore, it can be argued that the US did not lose this war; that the South Vietnamese did, once America withdrew its military action and funding had been cut off by Congress.

21.

This war, at its peak, was costing the US $2 billion each month. The South Vietnamese finally had been defeated by the North, who had remained supported and supplied by the Soviet Union and China.

LOADING CASUALTIES ONTO A HELICOPTER

CASUALTIES

During the Vietnam War, 2.59 million Americans served for their country. 58,307 of the US troops were killed and 304,000 wounded. 75,000 returned with severe disabilities. The number of amputations or crippling wounds were 300% higher than they were during World War II. One out of ten Americans that served in this war ended up as a casualty.

The average age of those troops that were killed during this conflict was 23. By the end of this lengthy conflict more than 3 million people were killed, including the more than 58,000 Americans. Over half of these casualties were Vietnamese civilians.

26

VIETNAM WAR DEFOLIATION MISSION A UH-1D HELICOPTER FROM THE 336TH AVIATION COMPANY SPRAYS AGENT ORANGE ON A DENSE JUNGLE AREA IN THE MEKONG DELTA

AGENT ORANGE

This became a hi-tech war for the Americans, using artillery, B52 bombers, helicopters, napalm, and defoliants that included Agent Orange and Agent Blue. Agent Orange was the chemical herbicide which the US forces sprayed to kill vegetation in the jungle as well as to infiltrate the Viet Cong hideouts during the time period of 1962 to 1971. The chemical Agent Orange (which came in orange containers) was utilized for chemical warfare during Operation Ranch Hand.

THE IMPORTANCE OF HELICOPTERS

This was the first war that saw such a large strategic deployment of helicopters. During World War II, the average soldier would see approximately 40 combat days during a four-year time period. During the Vietnam War, the average soldier saw approximately 240 combat days in one year; because of the mobility of a helicopter.

YAH-64 1982 01759-1 CR

The Bell UH-1 Iroquois, which had the nickname of "Huey", was utilized extensively during counter-guerilla operations. During this war, 7,013 Hueys were flown and 1,074 pilots were killed. The mobility that the Huey provided became crucial during the accurate and fast deployment of troops.

They were also used successfully in MEDEVAC and search and rescue tasks.

It was extremely dangerous to fly the helicopters as they were always visible to hostile fire, including their own base camps.

THE US PRESIDENTS

Four US Presidents served during the lengthy war. President Dwight D. Eisenhower and President John F. Kennedy each increased the number of American troops and military advisors to South Vietnam during the late 1950s and the early 1960s. President Lyndon Johnson then increased greatly the number of American military support until 500,000 US soldiers were now in Vietnam.

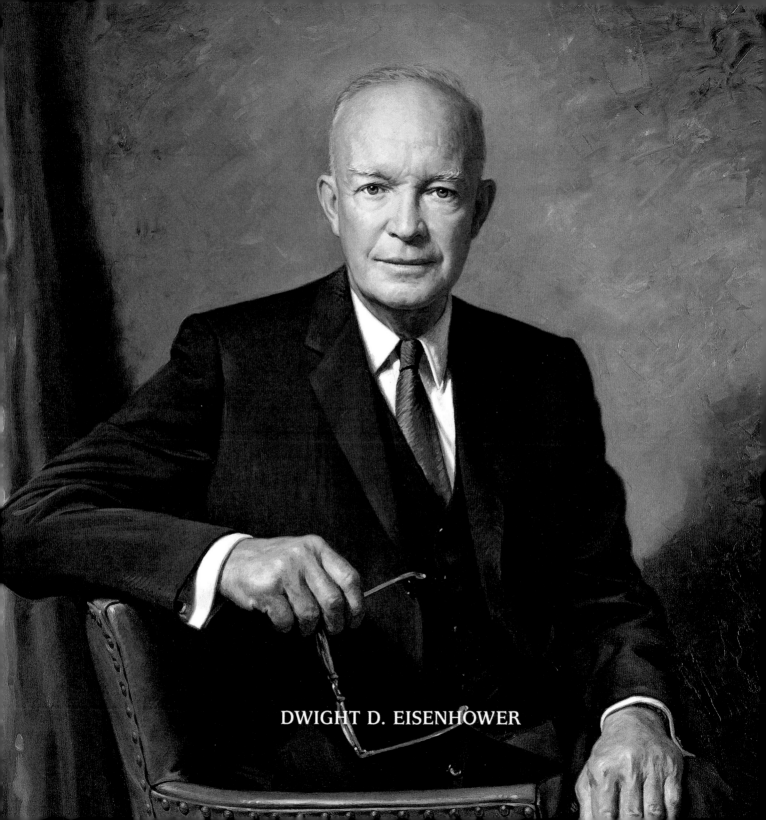

DWIGHT D. EISENHOWER

LYNDON B. JOHNSON

Distrust of President Johnson increased as the credibility gap grew between what the president and the military were telling the American public regarding the conflict and what the American media was reporting.

The Communists' Tet offensive became a severe setback for the US and reports of atrocities, including the My Lai massacre, increased the number of anti-war demonstrations in the United States and forced President Richard Nixon to decrease the troops in Vietnam and send Henry Kissinger, his secretary of state, for negotiation with North Vietnam for a cease fire. On August 15, 1973, direct military involvement by the US ended and South Vietnam was taken over completely in 1975 by the communists.

CHOLON AFTER TET OFFENSIVE
OPERATIONS 1968

WHAT WAS THE TET OFFENSIVE?

During Tet, the Vietnamese new year, on January 30, 1968, the Vietnamese launched a massive surprise attack. This attack was referred to as the "Tet Offensive" in which the North Vietnamese and the Viet Cong forces coordinated a series of attacks on over 199 south Vietnamese towns and cities, including an attack on the American Embassy in Saigon by the Viet Cong.

VIETNAM VETERANS MEMORIAL

During this same week, the number of American soldiers that were killed had surpassed that of the Korean War.

At this point, many Americans gave up any hope of winning the Vietnam War, and this was the beginning of the anti-war movement.

THE MY LAI MASSACRE

This massacre took place on March 16, 1968 and involved US soldiers killing somewhere between 347-504 unarmed South Vietnamese, consisting mostly of children, women, and old men.

47

MY LAI MASSACRE WOMAN
AND CHILDREN

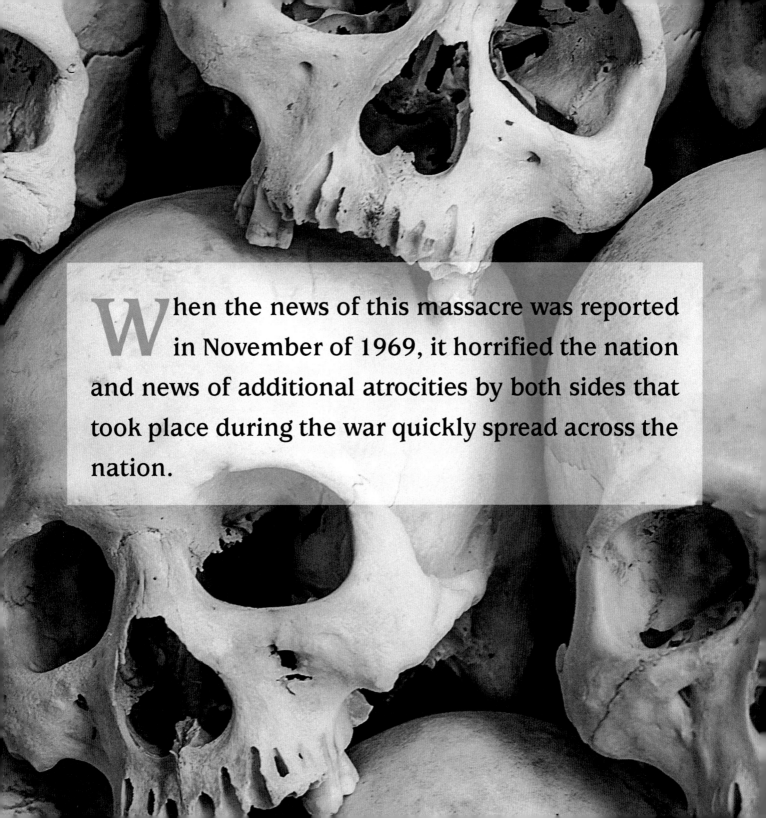

When the news of this massacre was reported in November of 1969, it horrified the nation and news of additional atrocities by both sides that took place during the war quickly spread across the nation.

There were even rumors about incidents that involved "fragging", which occurred when the discouraged American troops would kill their superior officers to avoid being sent on a dangerous mission.

US MARINES IN OPERATION

VIETNAM WAR
IN MEMORY OF

ADAMS, CARL TURNER

ANDERSON, JOHNNY MAC

ANDERSON, NORMAN RALPH

ARENAS JR., MANUEL V.

AYRES, JAMES HENRY

BAILEY, ELLIS M.

BASDEN, JERRY DON

BEAN, JIMMY DALE

BEARD, DONALD WAYNE

BEGGS, TERRY KENT

BERRY, VANCE ALYN

FREEMAN, JAMES P

FULKERSIN, ROBERT

FURPHEY, KENT PA

GAGE, NORMAN GL

GALBREATH, BOBB

GALVEZ, TOM

GARCIA, ROBERT

GEURIN, STEPHEN

GIBNER, GEORGE

GILBERT, JAMES C

GRAY, JAMES KEN

GREEN, JIMMY LE

THE VIETNAM WAR MEMORIAL

To honor the individuals of the American armed services that lost their lives during this conflict, there is a monument located in Washington, D.C. known as the Vietnam War Memorial. The names of this MIA (Missing in Action) or KIA (Killed in Action) are inscribed in the black marble wall of the Memorial.

Even though the United States did not win this war, it is still a major part of its history and there is much more information about it that has not been covered in this book.

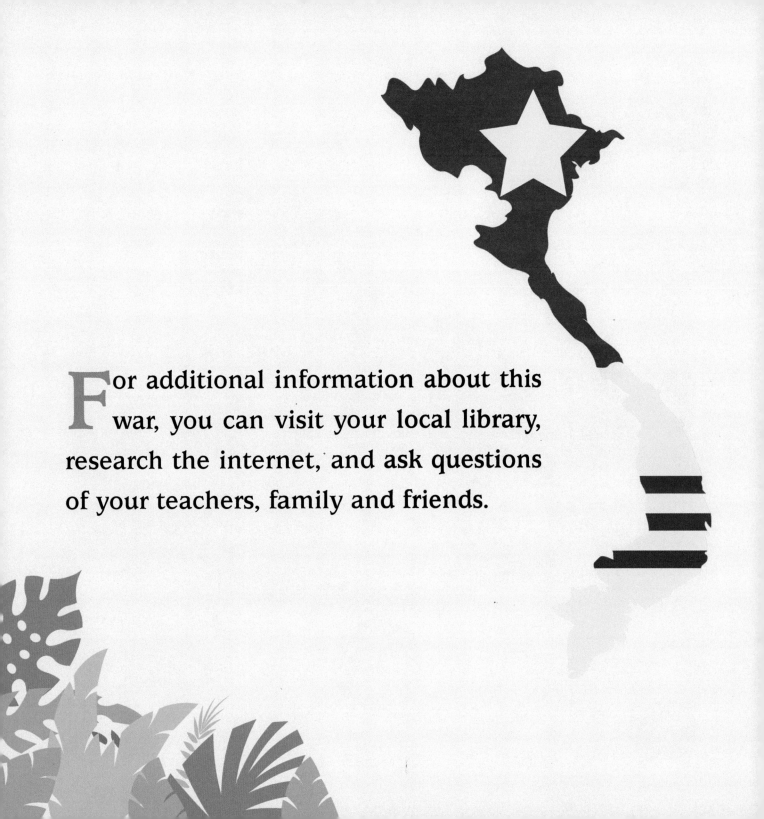

For additional information about this war, you can visit your local library, research the internet, and ask questions of your teachers, family and friends.

Visit

BABY PROFESSOR
EDUCATION KIDS

www.BabyProfessorBooks.com

to download Free Baby Professor eBooks
and view our catalog of new and exciting
Children's Books